WORDS of LIFE

William M Rumball

William M. Rumball

Kingdom Publishers

www.kingdompublishers.co.uk

Words Of Life

Copyright © William M. Rumball

All rights reserved.

No part of this book may be reproduced in any form by photocopying or any electronic or mechanical means, including information storage or retrieval systems, without permission in writing from both the copyright owner and the publisher of the book. The right of William M. Rumball to be identified as the author of this work has been asserted by him/her in accordance with the Copyright, Designs and Patents Act 1988 and any subsequent amendments thereto.
A catalogue record for this book is available from the British Library.

ISBN: 978-1-913247-36-2

1st Edition by Kingdom Publishers
Kingdom Publishers
London, UK.

Acknowledgment:

I especially acknowledge the formative influence of Hilda and Arthur in guiding me to a living faith and John and Peggy for their ongoing encouragement and witness.

You can purchase copies of this book from any leading bookstore or email
contact@kingdompublishers.co.uk

Contents

CHURCH AS COMMUNITY
The Fruits of the Spirit *4*
    The Serving Community *6*
    The Witnessing Community *6*
    The Suffering Community *7*
    The Family *8*
    Those in Authority *8*
    The Neighbour *8*
    Citizens of Heaven *9*
    Holiday Church *9*
    Refectory *12*
    Wounds *13*

PASTORAL
    Love's Secret *14*
    Solace uncertain *15*
    Silence *16*
    Gas, gaiters, crumpets and tea. *18*

WITNESS AND REVELATION
    Nativity *19*
    Epiphany *20*
    Candlemas Nunc Dimittis *21*
    Matins' Bell *21*
    Evensong *22*
    Resurrection *23*
    Peter is your Love True? *24*
    Peter, Peter, Peter *25*
    The Proof of Faith *26*
    The Offering of Life *26*
    Glimpses *28*
    The Master's mind. *28*

THE DIVINE
    The Way *29*
    Who is this Jesus? *29*
    'YHWH' *30*

William M. Rumball

CHURCH AS COMMUNITY

The Fruits of the Spirit

Paul's greatest fruit of love,
The nectared essence of above,
Carries all before high on the cross,
And gains all by selfless loss.

Joy shall ne'r be confounded,
As contentment fully rounded.
But darkest dungeon's depth all confused,
By saddest suffering sorrow now diffused.

The kiss of quiescent calm is peace,
As solid love's skilful artifice,
Unties the knitted mind's brow,
To unknot ache, relight shadow.

Patience the ever trustful virtue,
Grants to each and all time's due.
Never reckoning, never counting,
But always faults forgiving and retorts denying.

Kindness ever begets more kindness,
Beauty's most mannered tress,

Child of gentleness and grace,
Nature's most beloved face.

Though mischief's sourest foe to fore,
Goodness is sound right to its core,
Strikes terror into evil's eye,
Which to goodness has no reply.

Truth keeps soul's self sharp focussed
Precise as truth on truth embossed.
Constant, same always, never contrary,
Goodness today, tomorrow will never vary.

Lover is with loved never more soft,
Gentleness the breeze through trees aloft,
Delicate touch of murmured rustle,
Courteous, polite caring's careful.

Self-control's restrained passion,
Is studious fast discretion,
Intemperate spirit it does restrain,
To banish tongues thoughtless pain.

Sent fruitful Spirit, flood
Of peace, joy and love,
Overwhelms again Adam's earth,
By each fresh Pentecost's rebirth.

William M. Rumball

The Serving Community

Christ, bare, imprisoned, lost, hungry,
We too oftentime fail to see,
In those who people our daily life,
Neglected child, friendless neighbour, forlorn wife.

Paul said, Therese agreed,
For Christ's eye, hand and feet a need,
Still the Spirit embodiment requires,
Despite our human flesh which soon tires.

To be his Body is to truly serve,
As Christ's sinew, muscle, nerve,
Perfect freedom lowly or comely,
A member, blessed by his service only.

The Witnessing Community

The ways and wills of God lie all around,
Witnesses of his love in the world abound,
If we but understand what is his love,
As the true pure witness of his descending dove.

Creator, the cascade fountain's source,
The Son's stream of living water's course,
Poured out as blood-red fire of life,
Spirit's witness cancels psyche's strife.

Those by the Spirit's Gospel infected,
Are salt and spice, the hill city lit, elected,
Earth's life-giving light to caress,
With unbroken chain of love's witness.

The Suffering Community

What Job despaired to understand,
Peter adjured we accept as true,
whate'er life demand,
In pursuance of the Saviour's way,
Its full cost however dear
 in suffering, scorn or scourge,
It is the saviour's joy to pay.

What we hesitate to bear,
That for his love the world must hold dear,
So his grief we dare to share,
Then in his presence we may ever stay,
Together with those already there,
Gathered with him in the air,
To mark his triumphant final Day.

William M. Rumball

The Family

Born of the flesh we share Christ's blood brotherhood,
Those called by the Spirit are the family of God,
Not we understand the family of the good,
But kith by grace, kin by mercy tied,
Temporal yet to the eternal will allied.

Those in Authority

Pharaoh, Cyrus, Caesar
Ruled by the authority of God,
Pharaoh, Cyrus, Caesar
Sinned by the connivance of the other.

Peter, James, John and we
Empowered by Trinity of love,
Neighbour, monarch, child
Claim authority by his love.

The Neighbour

A neighbour's need can strike us blind to our blindness,
Too often life's hideous evokes from us very little kindness,
Lord Christ take pity, open our hearts and eyes,
To hear you and meet them in their sighs.

Citizens of Heaven

John's apocalyptic horrors appal and frighten,
The earthbound, no matter if we know how or when,
But John's glorious heavenly vision,
Inspires our hope of renewed creation.

To be numbered with the white clad hosts,
With lives sealed by the angel's toast,
Our sins first to the heavenly blaze revealed,
And so to the Lamb's cleansing blood we yield

Holiday Church

Amidst the churchyard tangle the church stands,
In almost studied neglect,
Among the smoothly finished lettered Welsh slate stones.
I wanted to know about this church,
It has two bells in the cote, unusual for such a place as this.
The door was locked. Neogothic, windows, Victorian buttressed porch,
Though, the barely legible plate at the gate said, an ancient foundation,
A medieval place of sanctuary and caring for the feeble and sick.

Here, a slight rise in a sheltered angle of the wall,
Permits me to peer through the latticed lead,
to see neatness, order and bright -red Wilton floor,
- yet no announcement beside the gate or door,
Of what the place is, or for,
This church stands quiet, nestled behind cottage row,
Apart somehow, forgotten by the secular flow,
With only ancient yews comfortable in its glance,
Mind, this settlement, though old, is small,
Populous only with the sheep on the adjacent slopes,
People are few and they only pass by the gate,
as it were by habit's accident.

When does this place worship,
- rise from undreaming sleep?
When feel the rush of human presence and hum
- the warm pulse of ecstatic prayer?
When will the Christ shine again in the strange sanctuary emptiness
- as the Spirit stirring in a beleaguered soul?

Next day, passing, I see the door unlocked,
What then today will this church be needed for?
Not worship, that's fortnightly Sundays,
And in Welsh, the caretaker person seems pointedly to say,
But offers no more to excite a desire to stay.
When later I return to probe inside this odd temple of man,
There is a veritable crowd assembled to monitor progress,

Of some new stained glass, a sign! of temporal progress if no other,
A marking, at least, of the passage of time.

Despite, however some noisy chatter and the busying artisan,
The mystery deepens when once I step inside I see,
All is in order, polish, tidy plaster walls,
Simple timber supports the sturdy single roof,
Bright embroidered pulpit and altar falls; but,
No sign of book, broom or bottle-gas,
No dog-eared funeral order or forgotten harvest poster,
In the gap beside the organ.
There is no magazine or pamphlet clutter, no
Rosta board, no music beneath the musician's seat.
There are two Bibles, on the lectern,
In Welsh, and a safe in the vestry, but
Which has though no discarded vestment or sign of use,
No artefact that breathes of any kind.
It is a sort of preserved, set in aspic, piece
Of non-existent history,
Sanitized and tidied for its reason's place.

Yet, this forlorn and lonely place, I later learn,
Was a place of brigands and the dark deeds,
Of dark centuries among the menacing watching hills;
Though nothing of this is felt, preserved or known,
Here, where all is tidied of human touch or life.

There is no lurking of anonymous lives in cobwebbed corners,
No liturgy breathes from the stones' pores,
Or hangs perceptibly in the air. There is no hint
Of man's vain-glorious battles, or pious frailties,
or mere dusty step of yesteryear.

But I know,
I felt,
God waits here, still,
patient to be heard,
and alone.

Refectory

They stand quiescent, before their place,
Before a grace becomes a tangible thing,
Sensibly nourishing but meagre, the plate,
Cradling the slenderly sufficient offering.

The meal's impedimenta rattle the end's,
Signal, concluding this affair of,
Heart's now crossed in gracious thanks and,
Borne away to some singular oblation.

In the centre of the table the dishes bear,
The faithfully rendered tithe as if left,
For an unseen guest, unseen yet felt,
Hand palpably poised in blessing there.

PASTORAL

Wounds

Maybe it's the faces uplifted,
Into the light of the preacher's gaze,
Or the downcast head the tension of,
The sinners' life betrays.

The still grips the all-meaning air,
And stirs brooding pains,
With brazen-bare all-pathos care,
And stirs yet another's pains,
Hidden, unknown and unsuspected
Sometimes I must grip hard the pulpit side,
Else I shrink sudden away,
From the deep-searing bloody cut opened wide,
By the stab of the word as it enters way deep inside,
With a scream of agony expressed,
In tortured look and faces pleading,
Showing hearts bleeding, bleeding, bleeding.

I bleed, I ache, I plead,
" O God why have you forsaken me "

William M. Rumball

Love's Secret

I must take out that chalice,
Which is a nothing whilst mouldering in a safe.
I must finger the pulse of its mottled mass,
Sense the throb of its existence,
Feel its history, decipher its secret sacred face.

I must take out that chalice,
That the people come to know it.
I must press it to their lips so they taste
Its past, its presence and its future promise, and be wet,
By its life-giving surge, its stirring,
Of the passions, of aching pangs,
Of emptiness presently to be met.

I must take out that chalice,
Its a guilty secret hidden fast away,
Before too scared, now let it arouse,
The din of my soul's cry,
To know and to be known,
By the Spirit of the living once unjustly dead,
And buried for convenience sake,
But now surely to emerge, resurrected,
That the people may be fed.

Solace uncertain

The priest offers solace, uncertain
Of source, effect or truth,
A priestly confidence trick of life's
Inevitability, the vulnerability,
Of love's hurt and hatred's honour,
Snatching rewards from the hungry mouths,
Of those waiting to regurgitate,
The comfort of digested experience.

Still the praise, still the spirit,
Of quiet, zest for living, loving,
The difficult, the diffident,
Who came, God knows why,
Who came, God knows why to him.

Silence the song, trim
The heart beat's flutter of,
Wings now afraid, becalmed,
Tremulous, frozen but knows,
Not why, God knows why, him

Smother the thought, the
Feeling's sense of the inappropriate,.
No kiss, no touch, no tingle,
To tease the stirring bowels of,
God knows why, not him

Still, silent the suffocating darkness,
Of life's nothingness,
At end, grave's bottom of it,
God knows why, him.

Silence

Not the silence which gathers menacingly as cold encircling fingers coiling and
    filling our inner space,
Not the silence which is the deep suffocating fathomless chill of the
    star-black sky collapsing down upon us,
No, nonesuch silence has, lapping, mingled with the discreet noisy pebbles
    and assorted flotsam of my day,
Rather is a soft warm rosy-fingered silence that's gathered itself
    to my waiting self.
At first, yes, the vacuum of absence waved seductively and clutched
    at a despairing me,
But then this silence warmed, warmed with thought of him in some
    office space or seated quiet in some public place with
    thought of me.
This silence is a faith of unknowing, a bright cloud of unreasonable love,

> blotting-out the dark heavier doubt of silence,
I've wanted to hear, wanted to know, wanted to touch,
> but instead I've heard just the silence,
Known only the steady pulse of my heart and touched that very knowing,
Of your Silence.

A reflection on Luke 23.43
> **'Today you will be with me in paradise'**

How do we see the long-time dead ?
Not those of a long gone era of course,
Rather my long-time dead,
In a time I'll not again live to see.

And how is it we who faithfully,
Shall spend this waiting time,
Of restful peace or peaceful nothingness,
Some blissful cacophony of congress ?

But I wait, I muse, I pray how can we see,
What has no shape, substance , ingress on nature ?
But then what in life that we take and contemplate,
Has singular shape, form, impress and weight ?

How can all mortal flesh of mind or matter,
Be heir to life's eternal covenant,
But then deny death's claim ?

What is its charm, its supreme majesty,
And where does its long-time mystery ever lie ?

Gas, gaiters, crumpets and tea.

They've made my Vicar a Bishop,
   that's what he wanted to be.
They've made my Vicar a Bishop,
   gas, gaiters, crumpets and tea.
They've made my Vicar a Bishop,
   well presented, lovely dresser you see.
They've made my Vicar a Bishop,
   Lord, Why ?,
You will your Church to be free,
   of gas, gaiters, crumpets and tea.
They've made my Vicar a Bishop,
   Lord, please explain it to me !

WITNESS AND REVELATION

Nativity

The nativity heralds a holy night,
Whilst Christmas promises naught at all.
The tinselled fripperies empty though bright,
Pale pointless beside the burden of the stall.

And Sun, Moon and stars outshone,
Before salvation's light did fall.

The Holy nativity is everything,
Merry Christmas is just fun,
It's the glory of God the angels sing,
Not the genius of any woman's son.

And Sun, Moon and stars o'ercome,
Are by God's love for ever won.

The nativity is everything,
Of which the earth and heavens ring,
Mere Christmas is shallow and sham,
The bright tinny ring of an empty can.

And Sun, Moon and stars return to their place,
In the magisterial cosmic plan.

Epiphany

    Magi considering the spinning earth,
    Wonder how we stand, even so
    Trembling firm upon its hurtling frame,
    Why some love and others are wracked with hate,
    Why some die sudden and too soon,
    Others peaceful in their beds,
    Why conflicts curdle earth's fitful peace,
    And evil's stain irrigates irretrievably,
    Tranquillity's virgin plain.
    So mysterious God's ponderous man
    Puzzles on divinity's mysterious plan.

    There is a secret and the secret,
    Simply put to westward Magi's search, that
    Here, beneath this star is life's all
    Disclosed, for life's living is life's secret
    Animating spark - the earth's secret,
    Is the secret, a thing which
    Is no mystery at all.
    God discloses to Magi and to man,
    What is not hidden though only faintly perceived,
    God is, what is, is just mysteriously so,
    Life is living, earth is spinning, lovers longing,
    Blackness overshadows all,
    But light floods the mind of the Magi.

Candlemas Nunc Dimittis

Lord thou lettest Simeon depart that day,
For he had seen the holy infant's future way,
Amidst the hoped for glory now revealed to all,
Dispelling Adam's conscious plight and fall.

According to your Word declared to this world,
Your blessed redemptive plan in him unfurled,
Just as insightful Magi's by night sky's kindly guide,
Declared Epiphany's glory will with mankind reside.

Pray Lord you grant us that holy saving sight,
My eyes to see the Christ-child's glorious light,
As revealed to Anna and Simeon that Holy Day,
Though heartbreak to come the blessed Virgin's way,

Lord bless the candle I light for you, and make me thine,
That I might greet the approaching solemn Lenten time,
Consoled and comforted by Jesus should I stray,
Oh Lord have this light cheer unholy me this holy holy day.

Matins' Bell

The morning drizzles with the monotonous beat
of rain and the Matins' bell.

Is this the constant prayer of saints ?
these tangled stems their bequest,
the soggy, bowed bouquets of creeping dampness
we're summoned to beyond above ?
Is dull-grey beat, the brain- sapped gloom,
the joy to which we're called ?
Or rather is this failed, sin-soaked thinness
the finger of Lazarus dipped in tepid gruel
Bent down to feed us, the drip and drizzle,
The authentic secret of which Saints would warn,
an incessant beat of law and prophets
- the only summons God will employ
Lest we trample down the Saints and the,
Spent, bent, beauty we utterly destroy.

Evensong

Prayers prayed,
The parson winds weary through stubble glebe,
Waif-feeble frail, bruise-wanded reed.
Then, caught unawares again by even's song
By lengthy light between others darkly throng,
Casting slough-shadows slash and stripe away,
Night confounded by slight the still summer's day,
Crossed by slanting sun-hatched glow,
Lined by level, ledge, hedge row-on-row,
An immaculate re-inception of the maker's inspired perfection.

Resurrection

" I've seen the Kingfisher ", I excitedly exclaimed
to my wife and the world last Easter-time, for
He who it seemed I never would know decided I now should see.
Though one evening before that Holy Week a local said,
The day would dawn, quite soon perhaps,
When the brilliant bronze and shimmering blue,
Who patrolled our water's way,
Would either or both succumb to factories' filth or village oaf,
- and alas poor me, I never having known Him.

I prayed next day after martin's bell,
That I be granted my first, and if needs be,
My one and only sighting.
So after prayers, but with little faith,
I turned down to the river.

And immediately, it seems, I came to the bank,
I saw the vague sparrow speck which winged my way,
At first a grey-black blob but which revealing his colours true,
Turned transformed and banked brilliant blue,
And flew in flaming arc.

My heart lept ! My heart sang " I have seen Him,
I have seen Him."

Then He alighted above the wear to rest close by His nest,
And His identity was clear.
So I immediately ran, ecstatic, up the hill,
To tell my wife that holy morn,
Just how it was that I had seen Him.

Oh, the magic of the thing !
- my doubting heart calling clear to Him,
He straightway came His marks to show me quite distinctly.
How could I think He'd leave me bereft, I never having known Him.

And now I've seen Him I see Him often,
Most usually when I don't expect or reckon,
Perhaps in my very soul as bread is blessed and broken,
Or else when I chance to walk His way,
Life's true flowing river;
When, again and again, at His discretion,
He comes to me,
Brilliant proof of His and our Resurrection.

Peter is your Love True?
John 21.1-14

Peter, Peter, Peter is your love true?
How secure the rock Galilee shore?

Can your God-breathed confession speak anew,
And we truly know what life's for.
Peter, Peter how do you show your love?
Will you love your Lord and feed his sheep?
As this divinely ordered from above,
And can we too his command now keep?
Peter, truly I must ask you once more,
Your loving friendship can it endure?
When prowl and roar of lions about beset
For betrayals deep which yet forget.

Peter, Peter, Peter

Peter, Peter, Peter, The Word implores,
From pebble beach where sea laps beneath air stilled silent skies,
Enfolding from the deep a stirring inner voice,
Of challenge, questioning perplexed emotion's seat.

Now impulse counters the mind's first recoil,
As faced by imagination's prowling beast,
The extent of love's demand to care and toil.

Peter between rock and this hard place,
Demurs at first, puzzled, afeared, unsure,
Dear Peter, beloved Peter, so sure Peter,
Confess, kiss, contemplate the very thought of Him,
To give all wherever you may be led,

For there lies the silver and the gold,
Of serene eternity and further shores,
Of the creation's destined glorious course.

The Proof of Faith

Assayer's Fire proves that gold is gold,
Whilst strongest steel is by flame tempered,
The testing fire proves faith is bold,
Cruellest test unflinchingly always answered.

Lord, burn out the clinging cankerous dross,
Which would disfigure and tarnish our love of you,
Lord, steel our frame with the imperishable cross,
And by emboldened hope our resolve renew.

Faith is by ease and riches never tempted,
Proved by trust's sound, sure and steely hold,
Though strongest steel is by flame tempered,
The assayer's fire proves gold is gold.

The Offering of Life

If life is properly invested,
A rich return is certain,
Talent never ever wasted,
Brings blessings in its train.

WORDS OF LIFE

Sinews stretched, nerves sparked and heart inflamed,
Are life's essential power-driving furnace fuel,
Sinews slack, nerves twitchless, heart lamed,
Are the stuff of living-death most cruel.

The Sprit stretches, sparks and enflames,
Christ's offer ripens fruitful fullness,
Eden's depository of faultless bliss,
Newly reveals the promise of his kiss.

William M. Rumball

THE DIVINE

Glimpses

Before me, between us, an obscuring,
Undergrowth's tangle and a painful briar's barricade,
Present themselves an impenetrable lattice
of material reality:
- yet triangled glimpses between of breathless symphonic order,
At one incomplete, incongruous, formed yet vague,
Are as the clear objective fact on the impressionist's canvas.
So I see you, peeping through where I let you,
Where I will you,
Shimmering clear blue in the mottled blur of disorder.

The Master's mind.

Words, philosophies are
hard to find,
for brilliant, star-spangled issue
seeking earth-bound dullness.

The Master's mind.
To comely comfort's
proud privilege blind,
Chose humility's self-scarred sacrifice,
Tempting our nature with eternal fullness.

The Way

You are he we must encounter,
He to whom we must then respond,
He who wills us to obey and agree,
To this meeting, this breathing of the same air,
This following you call love's domain.

Who is this Jesus?

Who is this Jesus, who looks down on me?
Eagle-eyed, yet he I can hide from,
When I chose him not to be,
My judge and executioner.

When afraid, he is my whistling in the dark,
Willing to materialize if really needed,
To emerge, ghostly,
Fear's stark shadows to dispel

When I need cause for dubious sentiment,
He's there with whispered text,
With which, strangulated, I circumvent,
Dishonestly my blasphemy.

When I need to bolster my flagging proclamation,
I dare to claim the promise of his Spirit,
The power of the world's creation!
To golden my squalid mean philosophy.

When I'm fearful because bemused,
By the sad thoughts of life and the sickly spell of death,
Then I cling ferociously to the nailed,
Saviour God of the Cross.

'YHWH'

I am 'I', not 'I am who I am'
for that is God,
And I am not that,
for if I were I would not doubt,
'I am who I am' but instead I am,
'what I am', not, 'who I am'.

www.ingramcontent.com/pod-product-compliance
Lightning Source LLC
Chambersburg PA
CBHW071551080526
44588CB00011B/1864